D1005955

MENAGERIE

MENAGERIE

SHARON MONTROSE

ILLUSTRATION AND LETTERING BY JULIANNA SWANEY

AN IMPRINT OF
HARPERCOLLINS*PUBLISHERS*

I think I could turn and live with animals, they are so pl

d self-contained, I stand and look at them long and long.

—Walt Whitman

Contents

Forest

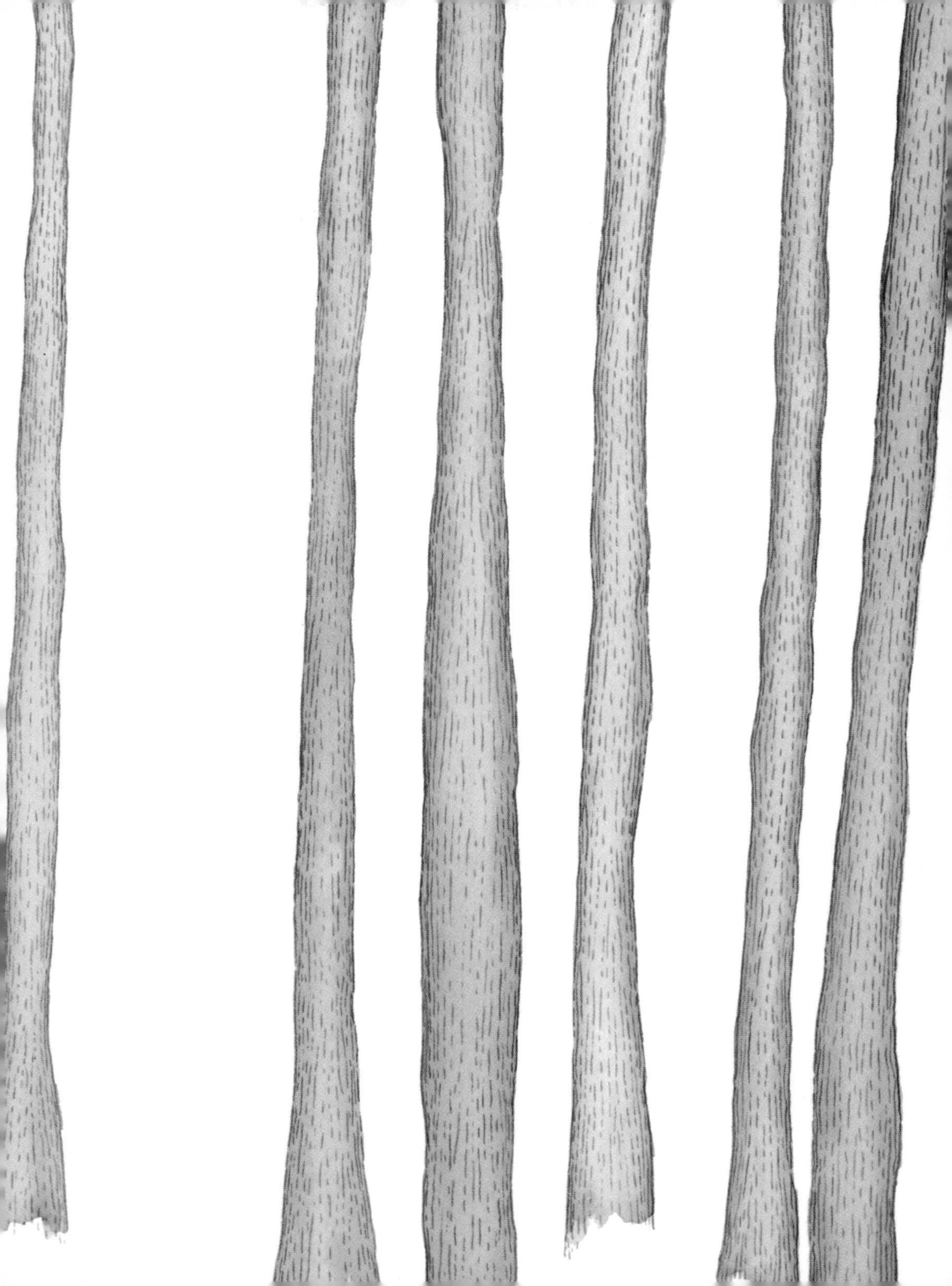

SOMEWHERE

There's

SOMEONE FOR ME

DEER ANTLERS ARE SHED EACH YEAR AFTER THE MATING SEASON AND BEGIN TO GROW ANEW IN THE EARLY SPRIN

BABIES

put your
HEAD
in the
clouds

Little Darlings

The Fox & The Hound

The day is better spent with you

smile

like you have nothing to prove

PRIMATES

Reptiles

BIRDS

Pretty in Pink

The World is my Home

FARM

JUST WAITING FOR THE GRASS TO TURN GREEN

AIN'T NOBODY HERE BUT US CHICKENS

CATS

Hoof

STAG

TIME
STANDS
STILL

The Animals

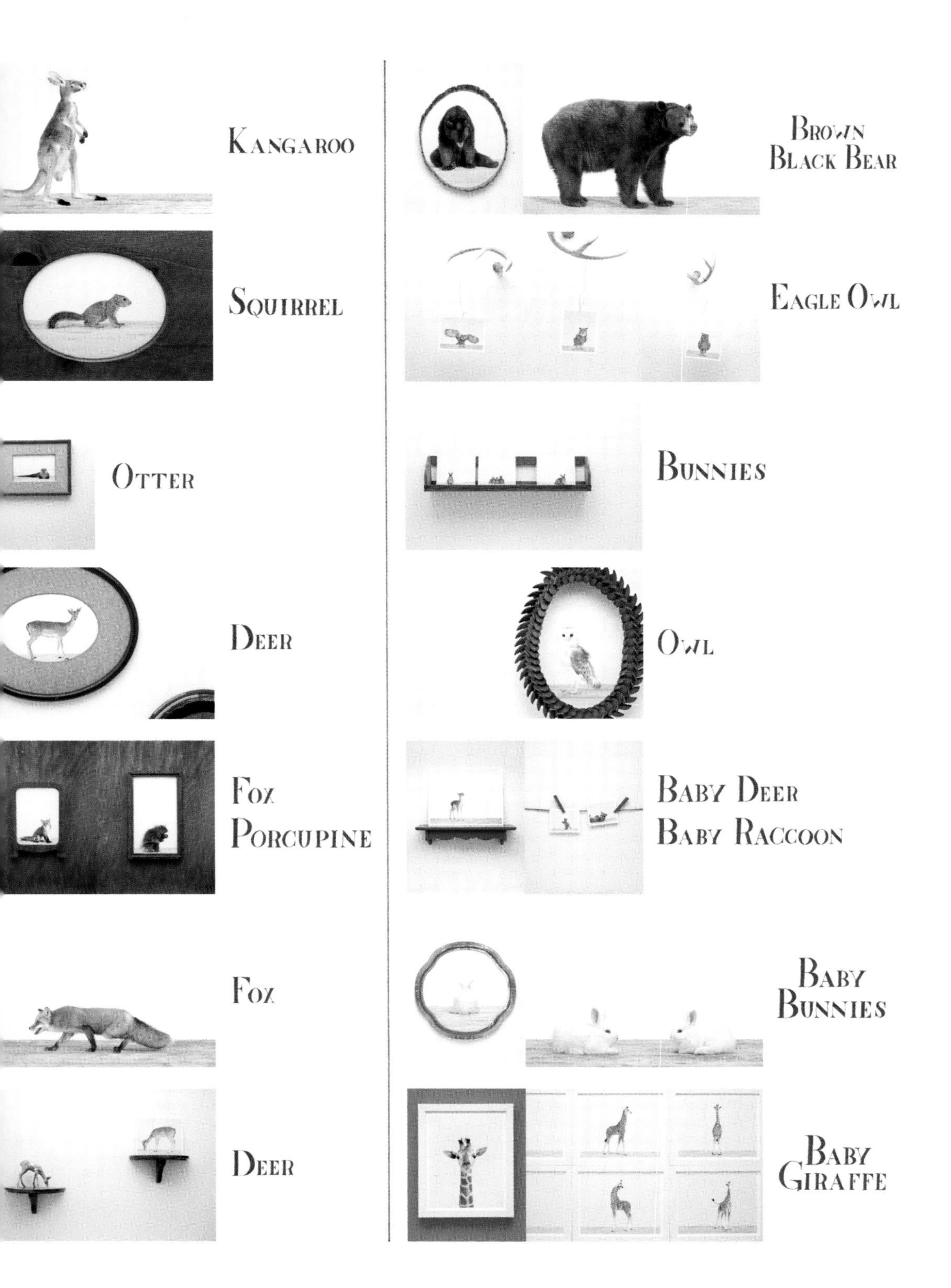
Kangaroo
Squirrel
Otter
Deer
Fox
Porcupine
Fox
Deer
Brown
Black Bear
Eagle Owl
Bunnies
Owl
Baby Deer
Baby Raccoon
Baby
Bunnies
Baby
Giraffe

Baby Bobcat
Lamb
Baby Monkey
Baby Fox
Baby White Tiger
Baby Kangaroo
Lion Cub

Baby
Zebra

Baby Goat

Baby
Porcupine

Baby
Donkey

Lion Cubs

Baby Fox

Basset Hound Puppy

Baby
Monkey

Baby
Kangaroo

Lamb

Baby Crane

Baby White Tiger
Baby Bobcat

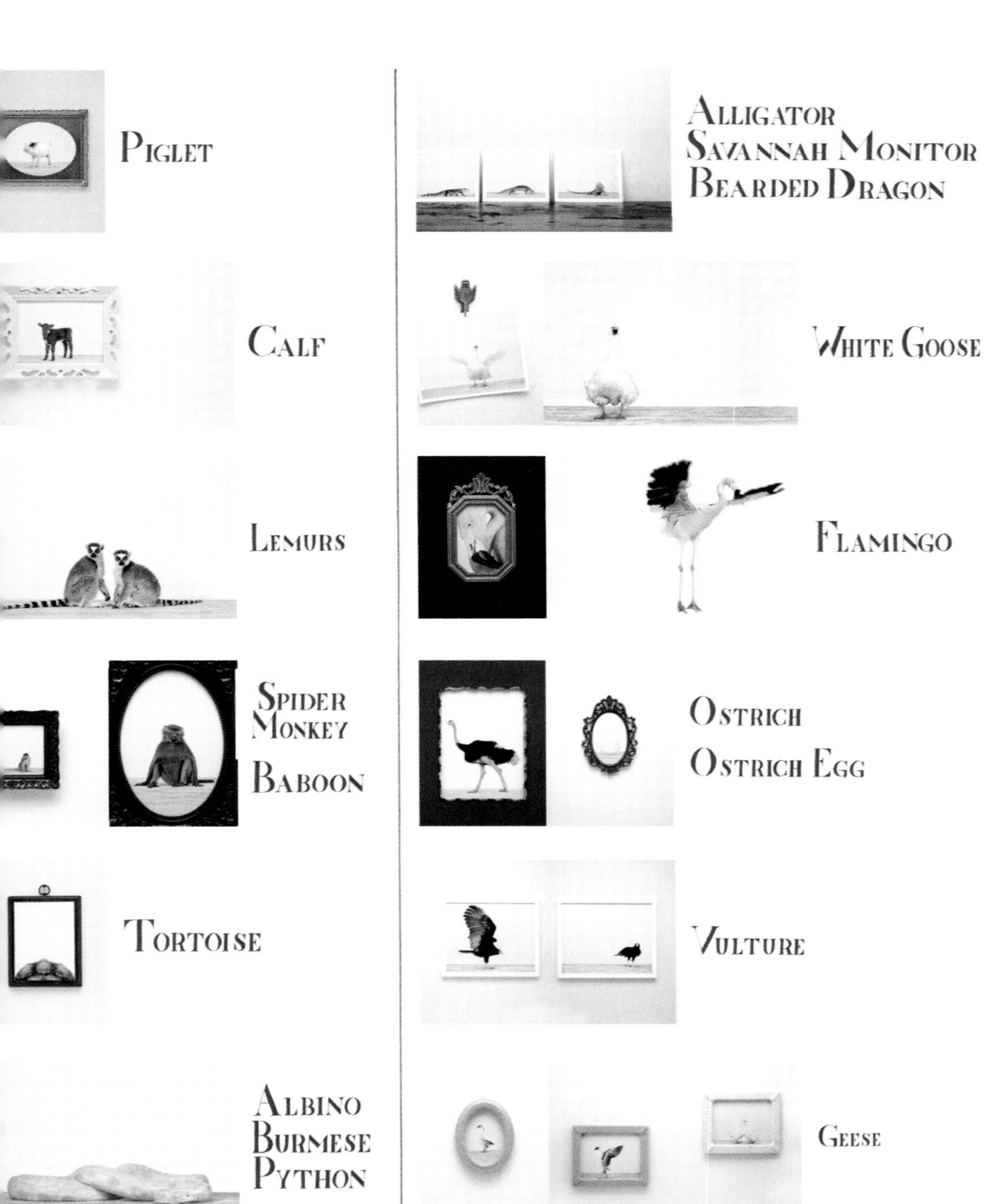
PIGLET
CALF
LEMURS
SPIDER MONKEY
BABOON
TORTOISE
ALBINO BURMESE PYTHON
ALLIGATOR
SAVANNAH MONITOR
BEARDED DRAGON
WHITE GOOSE
FLAMINGO
OSTRICH
OSTRICH EGG
VULTURE
GEESE

Trumpeter Bird

Pheasants

Macaw

Miniature Donkey

Cow

Pygmy Goat

Rabbits

Pony

Chicken
Roosters

Mule

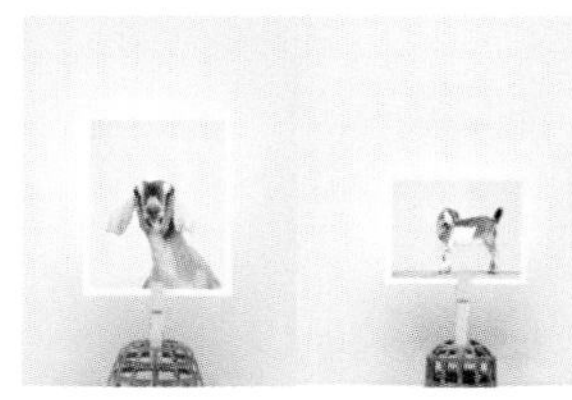

Nubian Goa

Pig

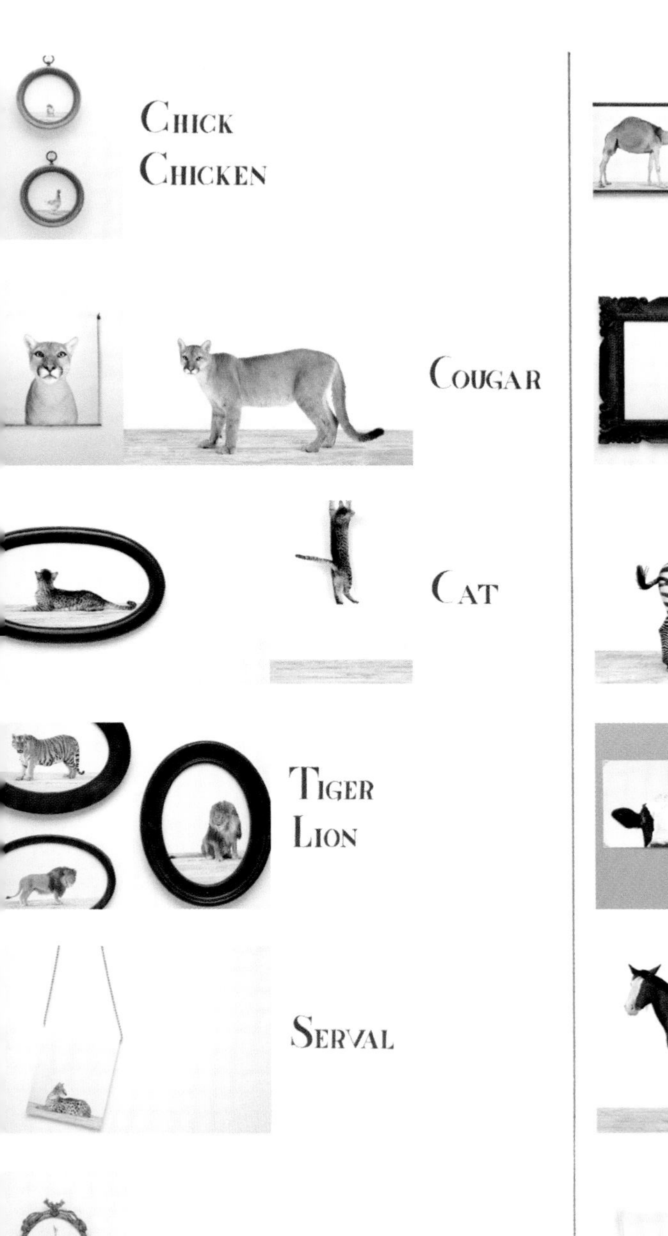

CHICK
CHICKEN
COUGAR
CAT
TIGER
LION
SERVAL
REINDEER

CAMEL
ZEBRA
ZEBRA
COW
DONKEY
CLYDESDALE
SHEEP

Resources

THE ANIMAL PRINTS SHOWCASED IN THIS BOOK
ARE AVAILABLE FOR PURCHASE THROUGH:
THE ANIMAL PRINT SHOP
WWW.THEANIMALPRINTSHOP.COM

ILLUSTRATIONS AND LETTERING:
JULIANNA SWANEY
WWW.OHMYCAVALIER.COM

WHITE GALLERY FRAMES:
WEST ELM
WWW.WESTELM.COM

YARN FRAMES (GRAY GOOSE):
KYLE SCHUNEMAN
WWW.LIVEWELLDESIGNS.COM

ANTLERS (EAGLE OWL):
ANTLER&CO
WWW.ANTLERANDCO.COM

VINTAGE FRAMES:
THRIFT STORES
WWW.ETSY.COM
WWW.EBAY.COM

Acknowledgments

I would like to extend my deepest gratitude to my amazing husband, Spencer Starr (I'm not easy to live with when I'm under book deadlines!), my editor, Cassie Jones (a true collaborative spirit), the talented and lovely Julianna Swaney (a total dream to work with), and my literary agent, Betsy Amster.

Also Joe Starr, Ann Livedalen, Lisa Lucas, Dara Siegel, Therese Newgard, Kim Lewis, Lorie Pagnozzi, Karen Lumley, Brian Toro, Dave Schafer, and all the dedicated animal handlers who lovingly care for these amazing animals as their own and ensured their welfare while being photographed.

A giant thank-you to the first person who blogged this series, Nichole Robertson (www.littlebrownpen.blogspot.com).

Also Joanna Goddard (www.joannagoddard.blogspot.com), Tina Roth Eisenberg (www.swiss-miss.com), Victoria Smith (www.sfgirlbybay.com), and all the other generous and countless blogs that have shared my work, along with everyone who has purchased prints.

You've all helped to make this book happen. You've helped me support organizations dedicated to animal rescue, educational programs, and nurturing wildlife. I humbly thank each and every one of you.

Melding her passion for photography with her love of animals, Sharon Montrose's definitive photographic style has made her one of the most sought-after commercial photographers specializing in animals. In addition to ten published photography books to her credit, Sharon shoots for some of the world's foremost pet industry brands. Her animal series photographs (featured in this book) are part of numerous public and private collections and have been awarded recognition by Communication Arts, Photo District News, The Art of Photography, hey, hot shot!, and the International Photography Awards. She lives in Los Angeles with her husband and two dogs. www.sharonmontrose.com

Julianna Swaney was born in Michigan and grew up playing outside with her dogs and cats, going on family vacations to historical sites, and going to antique stores, all of which continue to be an influence on her work. She attended Maine College of Art and got her BFA in 2005. She now makes a living from her artwork in Portland, Oregon. www.ohmycavalier.com

First Edition

Designed by Sharon Montrose
Illustrated by Julianna Swaney

ISBN 978-0-06-204920-9

11 12 13 14 15 [RRD] 10 9 8 7 6 5 4 3 2